Read & Respo

Ages
7–11

Read & Respond

Ages 7–11

Author: Jillian Powell

Commissioning Editor: Rachel Mackinnon

Development Editor: Rachel Coombs

Editor: Vicky Butt

Assistant Editor: Caroline Carless

Series Designer: Anna Oliwa

Designer: Liz Gilbert

Illustrations: Mike Lacey, Beehive Illustration

Text © 2011 Jillian Powell © 2011 Scholastic Ltd

Designed using Adobe InDesign

Published by Scholastic Ltd,
Book End, Range Road, Witney,
Oxfordshire OX29 0YD
www.scholastic.co.uk

Printed by Bell & Bain
1 2 3 4 5 6 7 8 9   1 2 3 4 5 6 7 8 9 0

British Library Cataloguing-in-Publication Data
A catalogue record for this book is available from the British Library.

ISBN 978-1407-12627-2

Acknowledgements

The publishers gratefully acknowledge permission to reproduce the following copyright material: **Hachette Children's Books** for the use of text extracts and the cover from *How to Train Your Dragon* by Cressida Cowell, first published in the UK by Hodder Children's, an imprint of Hachette Children's Books, 338 Euston Road, London, NW1 3BH. Text and illustrations © 2003, Cressida Cowell (2003, Hodder Children's Books).
Every effort has been made to trace copyright holders for the works reproduced in this book, and the publishers apologise for any inadvertent omissions.

How to Train Your Dragon

About the book

Cressida Cowell's childhood fascination with Vikings and dragons gave her the idea for *Hiccup the Viking Who Was Seasick*, a picture book about a little Viking boy who gets seasick and is scared of everything, but conquers his fears to save the day. This book became the inspiration for *How to Train Your Dragon*, the first in a series of stories about Hiccup and his Viking adventures. With their combination of Viking legend and fantastical dragons, the author has described the stories as 'fantasy books pretending to be history books'.

How to Train Your Dragon has all the key elements of a classic adventure story: an unlikely young hero who, when put to the test, overcomes his fears and handicaps to save his tribe; a wild and dramatic setting fraught with challenges and dangers; and plenty of cliffhangers to keep the reader turning the page. Hiccup cannot become a full member of his tribe unless he passes the Dragon Initiation Test and proves that he can train a dragon to hunt for him. Handicapped by an unusually small and toothless dragon, he fails the test along with his peers when their dragons begin fighting, dooming the boys to exile. But a bigger challenge awaits: a gigantic Sea Dragon has woken up and is threatening to terrorise the island of Berk. Only Hiccup, whose nerdish pastime of studying dragons has taught him their language, has the skill to outwit the Sea Dragon and save his people. Overall, this is a 'coming of age' story about a boy who finally finds the hero within himself, told in an engaging and humorous style abounding with jokes.

About the author

Cressida Cowell grew up in London and on a small Scottish island where her family spent their summer holidays. As a child, she became fascinated by her father's stories about the Vikings who had invaded the island archipelago 1200 years before, and local legends of dragons that lived in the caves in the cliffs. Cressida began writing her own stories about the dragons and drawing pictures of the different species she imagined.

At school, her favourite subjects were English, History and Art. She went on to study English at university before training for a BA in graphic design at St Martin's School of Art and an MA in narrative illustration at Brighton. For her final project at art school, she created a picture book called *Little Bo Peep's Library Book* which was published in 1998. She went on to write ten more picture books, including the *Emily Brown* stories, the first of which (*That Rabbit Belongs to Emily Brown*) won the Nestlé Children's Book Prize in 2006. By now, she was writing and illustrating stories for older children, publishing the first of the *Hiccup* series in 2003.

Cressida Cowell lives in London with her husband and three children and is a keen book collector.

Facts and figures
How to Train Your Dragon was first published in 2003.
It has been translated into 30 languages.
It was adapted into a DreamWorks film in 2010.
Eight more titles in the series have since been published.

Guided reading

First impressions

Look together at the cover of the book. Ask: *What does the title suggest? What does the illustration suggest?* (The title echoes 'How to' instruction manuals; the design suggests an old, leather-sewn 'tome'; the dragon suggests fantasy – some may spot the detail of the Viking helmet suggesting setting/characters.)

Next, read the back-cover blurb and ask what more we learn about the story. (It is set on an island called Berk; the main character is a young Viking called Hiccup; he is going to fight a dangerous dragon and must become a hero.)

Find out what the children already know about the Vikings. Ask: *Where and when did the Vikings live?* Establish some basic facts. (The Vikings came from the lands now known as Scandinavia circa 700–1100CE; they were great warriors and adventurers; they sailed in longships with fantastical beasts like dragons and serpents on the prows.)

Ask: *What kind of story about the Vikings do you think this will be?* (History, fantasy, adventure.) Scan through the chapter headings and note design features such as the ink blots, doodle drawings and changes in font. Ask the children what these suggest about the book. (It is going to be a fun read; it might be funny and have jokes in as well as telling an exciting adventure.)

Scene setting and characters

The first reading should be used to familiarise the children with the storyline and introduce the characters and key themes. Before you begin reading, look briefly at the character drawings and names as well as the maps that preface the book. Encourage the children to note the humour in character names like *Clueless* and *Dogsbreath*, and in place names such as *Pointy Point* and *Meathead Graveyard*.

Read the preface. Ask: *Whose story is this?* (It is going to be looking back at the childhood of a Viking Hero called Hiccup.)

Read the first chapter. Pause to ask the children what it is the boys have to do and why. (They have to catch their own baby dragon and train it for their initiation into the tribe.) Check that they understand the meaning of 'initiation'. (Passing tests or going through a ritual/ceremony to become a full member of a group or tribe.) Ask them why Hiccup is to be in charge and why it is such a challenge for him. (He is the son of the Chief, but the other boys regard him as useless and incompetent.)

Read on, pausing to establish the dynamics in the class of boys: the bullies – Snotlout and Dogsbreath, and the bullied – Hiccup and his best friend Fishlegs. Continue to the end of Chapter 2. Ask: *What have we learned about Hiccup?* (He is the Chief's son, is small and puny, gets bullied, but shows bravery in the task and also selflessness in giving Fishlegs his dragon.) *What is the hook or 'page turner' at the end of this chapter?* (We want to know what kind of dragon Hiccup has got hidden in his dragon basket.)

Plot lines

Read on through Chapter 3, pausing to ask: *What is the next challenge that the boys are working towards?* (The Thor'sday Thursday Celebrations when they must show that they have successfully trained their dragons.)

Continue reading to the end of Chapter 4. Ask the children to pinpoint some of the humour. (The idea of the scrawny, little, toothless dragon that Hiccup has to try to train; the joke of the library book which is written by a renowned expert and has gushing reviews but contains only three words, *Yell at it*.)

Read through Chapter 5. Ask: *What does Old Wrinkly foretell for Hiccup and the future of the tribe?* (He believes Hiccup will achieve great things and that it will not be through brute force, but by being cunning and clever and having knowledge of dragons.) Briefly review one of the key 'hooks' of the plot line – how Hiccup, who is seen as weak and useless by his peers, will overcome his fears to become a hero.

Continue reading to the end of Chapter 9. Ask the children to consider the main thrust of

Guided reading

the plot line here – whether Hiccup will get the mischievous and unruly Toothless trained in time so that he can pass his initiation. Ask: *What skill does Hiccup possess that gives him an advantage?* (He can speak Dragonese.) *What incentive seems to work best with Toothless?* (Promising to tell him jokes if he manages to catch fish.)

Read Chapter 10. Ask the children to summarise what happens at the celebrations and what the consequences are. (Toothless incites a dragon fight and the boys fail the test, which means they will be sent into exile.)

Read on to the beginning of Chapter 12. Ask the children what has happened and how this can change the fate of Hiccup and the exiled boys. (A giant Sea Dragon has been woken by the storm and is threatening the people of Berk; Hiccup is the only one who knows Dragonese so now the island's fate depends on him.)

Happy endings

Continue reading to the end of Chapter 14. Ask: *Can you explain what Hiccup's cunning plan is?* (To use their dragons to infuriate the giant Sea Dragons and incite them to fight and kill each other.) *What is the 'page turner' at the end of Chapter 15?* (The Green Death is wounded but still alive and intent on killing them all.)

Read on to the end of the book. Discuss how Hiccup is saved from a terrible fate by little Toothless and his own initiative. (Toothless makes the Sea Dragon sneeze and Hiccup has blocked the fire holes in its throat, so it explodes when it tries to breathe fire.) Ask: *What makes this a good/satisfying ending?* (Hiccup and his little dragon prove everyone wrong: the underdogs become the heroes, saving the whole island from a terrible fate.) Consider the epilogue and remind the children that the story began with a note from Hiccup. Ask: *What do we learn has changed now that Hiccup has grown up?* (He has become a famous hero; the great Sea Dragons are no longer seen and are already becoming the stuff of myth and legend, as they are to us.)

Second reading

Use subsequent readings to allow the children to explore in more depth some of the key features and ideas in the novel. As they already know the storyline, they can now concentrate on different aspects, such as the setting, text features and language/word play.

Structure

Divide the text into sections that reflect the structure of the plot:
● First challenge – catching a dragon, Chapters 1–3.
● Second challenge – training a dragon, Chapters 4–10.
● Third challenge – fighting the Sea Dragons, Chapters 11–19.

Note how Chapter 6 foreshadows later events by introducing the slumbering Sea Dragon. Introduce the term 'foreshadowing' and explain that this is a device that authors use to prepare for or lead up to a later episode in the story.

Encourage the children to consider how everything in the plot is leading up to the Thor'sday Thursday Celebrations. The day appears to end in failure; then fate intervenes and gives Hiccup the chance to redeem himself and the other boys, saving them from exile and the whole island from destruction.

Note together how the story is 'topped and tailed' by the note and epilogue by Hiccup. Discuss how the book can be seen as Hiccup's memoirs/autobiography as well as being in the tradition of bards' tales of Viking history and battles. It can also be seen as another version of the 'how to' book by Professor Yobbish which features in the plot.

Style

As you read, look at the drawings and encourage the children to appraise the childlike style of the scribbled notes, ink blots and doodles. Ask: *What do the drawings contribute to the story?* (They add to the humour; they bring the text alive as if it is a 'work in progress', like an exercise book full of ink splodges and torn paper.)

Note the frequent changes in text font and how they are used. For example, a quaint font is used to differentiate Dragonese, and capital letters are used to indicate Gobber's booming voice. Pause also to consider how different text features are woven into the narrative, such as the encyclopaedic entries for the dragon species, letters written (in poor English) by characters, and the book within the book by Professor Yobbish.

Setting

Encourage the children to think about how the wild, stormy setting contributes to the plot and atmosphere. For example, the bleakness of the landscape – with its rugged cliffs and the cold snow and winds – makes the challenges the boys face all the harder. The storm that brews on Thor'sday Thursday builds tension and drama and it also wakes up the Sea Dragons, leading to Hiccup's greatest challenge.

Themes

When they have finished re-reading the text, ask the children to reflect on some of the key themes: adventure; friendship; overcoming fears and bullies; the idea that intelligence, understanding and knowledge can be more valuable than brute force.

Shared reading

Extract 1

● Read an enlarged copy of Extract 1. Ask: *What is the boys' mission?* (They must each catch a dragon while it is hibernating in the caves.) Ask the children to explain what makes the situation so dangerous. (If the dragons wake, they could tear them to pieces.)

● Ask the children to describe the cave. (Dark, damp, cold, smelly.) Circle the words *claustrophobic, stench, in unison, penetrate* and *vibrate*. Ask the children to explain what they mean and think of other words that could replace them.

● Underline words that suggest how difficult/ uncomfortable the boys' task is: *clammy, claustrophobic, squirming, crawling*.

● Ask: *Which words tell us how Hiccup is feeling?* (He is sweating; his stomach is churning – but he remains resolute in his task.) Can the children recall other episodes when Hiccup conquers his fears? (When he confronts the Green Death/ inside its mouth.) What does this tell us about him? (He is an ordinary boy but he is brave.)

● Focus on the dragon pulse. Ask: *Can you remember other ways that dragons can affect humans?* (Their hypnotic gaze; synchronising pulses when they are digesting humans.)

Extract 2

● Read an enlarged copy of Extract 2. Ask the children to gauge the pace of this episode: *Is it fast or slow? What makes it exciting?*

● Suggest that in fast-paced episodes, strong action verbs are important. Invite the children to pick out all the past-tense action verbs and circle them: *scrambled, landed, bashed, flapped, replaced, swooped, whirled, threw, soared, hit*.

● Next, circle or underline verbs in the participle form: *slipping, sliding, shrieking, savaging, sinking, ripping, pouring, shooting, melting, spinning, killing, landing, disappearing*. Ask the children to try replacing some of the participles with simple past-tense verbs. Discuss how this changes the effect: 'Fire shot from their nostrils and melted the snow before them.'

● Reflect on how the participle form creates immediacy, suggesting continuous action.

● Circle words describing the terrain and ask the children to explain them: *gully, gorge, cliffs, canyon*. Ask: *How would you describe this kind of landscape?* (Coastal, island, bare, rocky, barren.)

● Locate the simile: *like the spines on a sea urchin*. Consider what makes it appropriate in this particular setting. (Berk is an island; the boys are familiar with marine animals.)

Extract 3

● Read Extract 3. Ask the children if they can identify two text types – report and narrative. Can they pinpoint the words where the text shifts? The first two paragraphs are in the style of a non-chronological report. From *Now both Dragons…* the text becomes narrative, with proper names and past-tense verbs.

● Challenge the children to add another sentence about Sea Dragons from their knowledge of the text. For example, 'They have fire holes inside their throats from which they breathe fire'.

● Ask the children to pick out an example of alliteration: *grim gurgles*.

● Underline the capital letters in the extract. Ask: *Why have they been used?* Focus on the deadly grips – *Throatchoker Grip* and *Breathquencher Hug* – and challenge the children to invent others, encouraging them to use alliteration: 'Suffocating Squeeze' or 'Grappling Grasp'.

● Consider sentence length, underlining the shortest sentence: *There was silence*. Analyse the impact of the very short sentences.

Extract 1

The tunnel was dripping and clammy. At times it was high enough for the boys to walk upright. Then it would close down into narrow, claustrophobic holes that the boys could only just squeeze through, squirming on their stomachs, with the flares held in their mouths.

After ten long minutes of walking and crawling into the heart of the cliff, the stench of dragon – a salty stink of seaweed and old mackerel heads – got stronger and stronger, until finally it became unbearable and the tunnel opened out into a ginormous cavern.

The cavern was full of more dragons than Hiccup could ever have imagined existed.

They were every possible colour and size, and they included all the species that Hiccup had heard of, and quite a few more that he hadn't.

Hiccup started sweating as he looked around him at pile after pile of the animals, draped over every available surface; even hanging upside-down from the roof like giant bats. They were all fast asleep, and most of them were snoring in unison. This was a sound so loud and so deep that it seemed to penetrate right into Hiccup's body and vibrate around his soft insides, churning his stomach and bowels, and forcing his heart to beat at the same slow dragon pulse.

If one, just *one*, of these countless creatures were to wake up, it would raise the alarm to the others and the boys would meet a horrible death. Hiccup had once seen a deer that had wandered too close to Wild Dragon Cliff torn to pieces in a matter of minutes…

Hiccup closed his eyes. 'I will NOT think about it,' he said to himself. 'I WILL NOT.'

SCHOLASTIC
www.scholastic.co.uk

READ & RESPOND: Activities based on How to Train Your Dragon

Extract 2

The boys scrambled over the slimy pebbles at the edge of the beach and back up Madman's Gully, the gorge they had climbed through a couple of hours before. This was a narrow crack in the cliffs filled with large rocks. They tried to move as quickly as they could, but this is difficult when you are slipping and sliding over huge stones covered in ice, and they made painfully slow progress.

A dragon that *hadn't* been put off by the snow came shrieking down into the gorge. He landed on Wartihog's back and started savaging him, sinking his fangs into Wartihog's shoulder and ripping red lines into his arms. Gobber bashed the dragon on the nose with the handle of his axe, and the dragon let go and flapped away.

But a whole wave of dragons replaced him, pouring into the canyon with awful, rasping cries, fire shooting from their nostrils and melting the snow before them, talons spread wickedly as they swooped downward.

Gobber stood, legs wide apart, and whirled his big, double-headed axe. He threw back his great, hairy head and yelled a terrible primeval Yell, that echoed down the sides of the gorge and made the hairs on the back of Hiccup's neck stick straight up like the spines on a sea urchin.

Individually, dragons tend to have a healthy sense of self-preservation, but they are braver when they hunt in packs. They knew now that they had the advantage of massive numbers, so they didn't check their flying for an instant. They just kept on coming.

Gobber let go of the axe.

Spinning end to end, the axe soared up through the softly falling snow. It hit the biggest dragon of the lot, killing him instantly, and then carried on going, landing in a snow-drift hundreds of feet away and disappearing.

Text © 2003, Cressida Cowell.

Extract 3

The Sea Dragon is the most well-defended creature that has ever lived on this planet. Its skin is over three feet thick in places, and so encrusted with shells and barnacles that it almost has the effect of armour.

It is also the most well-armed creature that has ever lived on this planet and its razor sharp claws and teeth can rip open its own iron crust as if it were made out of paper…

Now both Dragons had terrible wounds, and their green lifeblood was pouring out of them.

The Green Death gripped the Purple Death around the neck with a deadly Throatchoker Grip.

The Purple Death hugged the Green Death around the chest with a deadly Breathquencher Hug.

Neither would let go – and the grip of a Dragon is a terrible thing. They reminded Hiccup of a picture on one of his father's shields: of two dragons forming a perfect circle as they ate one another, each with a tail in their mouth.

The Dragons thrashed around wildly in the surf, gagging and choking, with their eyes popping, their tails causing such tidal waves that the boys were soaked, even though they were scrambling away from the Headland as fast as they could.

Finally, with some last heaving shudders and grim gurgles, both mighty beasts lay still in the water.

There was silence.

The boys stopped running. They stood gasping for breath, watching the motionless beasts with dread. The boys' dragons, which were flying some way ahead of the boys, also turned, and hung still in the air.

The Terrible Creatures didn't move.

The boys waited two long minutes, as waves lapped gently over the great, motionless bodies.

'They're dead,' said Thuggory at last.

Text © 2003, Cressida Cowell.

Plot, character and setting

The Vikings

> **Objective:** To interrogate texts to deepen and clarify understanding and response.
> **What you need:** Copies of *How to Train Your Dragon*, flip chart, photocopiable page 15.
> **Cross-curricular link:** History.

What to do

● Tell the children that they are going to focus on how the author uses Viking history and legend.
● Briefly recap who the Vikings were, and where and when they lived. (They lived in the lands now known as Scandinavia circa 700–1100CE; were great warriors and adventurers; sailed in longships.) Ask the children to volunteer any facts they know about the Vikings and write them on the flip chart.
● Next, ask if they can suggest what we learn about Vikings in the book that might be based

on historical fact. (They had gods called Thor and Woden; lived in tribes; were skilled hunters, fishers and warriors; burned boats for funeral ceremonies.) Write their suggestions on the board.
● Hand out photocopiable page 15. Tell the children to scan the novel and work in pairs to fill in the boxes.
● Discuss which aspects of the story are based on historical fact and which are not. (The Vikings missed the Romans by about 300 years; horned helmets were only for ceremonial occasions; there were no dragons.)

> **Differentiation**
> **For older/more confident learners:** Ask pairs to use books/the internet to decide whether the things listed on the photocopiable sheet are based on fact.
> **For younger/less confident learners:** Complete the photocopiable sheet as a shared activity.

A real adventure

> **Objective:** To identify and summarise evidence from a text to support a hypothesis.
> **What you need:** Copies of *How to Train Your Dragon*, flip chart, individual whiteboards and pens.

What to do

● Ask the children: *Which genre do you think the story fits into? Why? Is it realistic, fantasy, comedy, adventure?* Elicit that there are elements of fantasy (the dragons), comedy (the story is full of jokes and comic events) and adventure (a hero on a personal quest).
● Focus on the term 'adventure' and ask the children to suggest ingredients for an adventure story. List their ideas on the flip chart. (A likeable hero; a trial or quest; a wild, dramatic setting full of risk and danger; a series of trials or tests that the hero has to overcome; an initial, exciting hook and cliffhangers which make the reader want to read on.)
● Arrange the children in pairs. They should

now think about how the novel matches up to the adventure checklist. For example, Hiccup faces trials – to catch and train a dragon and to defeat the Sea Dragons. They should note down their ideas on their whiteboards.
● When they have finished, consolidate their ideas on the flip chart.
● Encourage the children to cite other adventure stories they have read, and reflect on what makes this one different. (Comedy, funny words and names; the mix of history and fantasy; the scribbled illustrations.)

> **Differentiation**
> **For older/more confident learners:** Challenge pairs to create a checklist for a humorous novel and a fantasy novel, and decide to what extent *How to Train Your Dragon* fits into those genres.
> **For younger/less confident learners:** Ask pairs to discuss which aspects make the story a comedy, and which make it a fantasy.

Plot, character and setting

The island of Berk

> **Objective:** To understand how writers use figurative and expressive language to create images and atmosphere.
> **What you need:** Copies of *How to Train Your Dragon*, photocopiable page 16, flip chart, individual whiteboards and pens.
> **Cross-curricular link:** Geography.

What to do

● Read together Chapter 3 as far as *the salty wastelands of Berk*. Ask: *What do we learn about the island of Berk? Can you describe the landscape and weather?* (Rocky gorges, cliffs, boggy land, bracken-covered hills; gales, snow and rain.) Write some of the suggestions on the flip chart.

● Let the children work in pairs to scan the story for any other features of the island. They should write down their findings on their whiteboards.

● Bring the class together and ask the children for suggestions to add to the flip chart.

● Tell them that they are going to fill in a page about Berk for a visitors' guide. Hand out photocopiable page 16 and ask the children to fill it in, working in pairs or individually.

● Discuss the setting in the context of the book. Ask: *Is the setting an important feature? How?*

> **Differentiation**
> **For older/more confident learners:** Challenge pairs to write a bulleted list of ways in which the setting is important to the story. (For example, it makes the boys' trial harder; the island is invaded by Sea Dragons.)
> **For younger/less confident learners:** Ask the children to draw and label a picture of Berk showing what the scenery is like.

Death or glory

> **Objective:** To interrogate texts to deepen and clarify understanding and response.
> **What you need:** Copies of *How to Train Your Dragon*, flip chart, individual whiteboards and pens.

What to do

● Ask the children to think of all the dangers that Hiccup faces in the story. List their suggestions on the flip chart in a random order. Then work through the list together, numbering the items in the order they appear in the plot.

● Arrange the class into pairs. Challenge the children to work through the list of dangers, deciding in each case who or what helps Hiccup to escape the danger. For example, when Hiccup is in danger of being swallowed by the Sea Dragon, the Roman spear stuck in its throat saves him. They can list their ideas on their whiteboards.

● Bring the class back together and ask pairs to share their ideas, writing them on the flip chart against each danger. For example:
  ● Danger – Hiccup may be impaled by the Sea Dragon's tooth;
  ● What saves him – Stoick's shield.

● Discuss how the dangers that Hiccup faces maintain a fast-moving and exciting plot.

> **Differentiation**
> **For older/more confident learners:** Let pairs discuss the extent to which Hiccup controls his own destiny. For example, is Toothless' act of bravery down to Hiccup's caring treatment of the little dragon?
> **For younger/less confident learners:** Let pairs discuss what they think are the worst or scariest moments in Hiccup's life and why.

Plot, character and setting

Heroes and hooligans

> **Objective:** To deduce characters' reasons for behaviour from their actions.
> **What you need:** Copies of *How to Train Your Dragon*, photocopiable page 17.
> **Cross-curricular link:** PSHE.

What to do

● Read Chapter 5 at pace. Ask the children to summarise what the leader of the Hairy Hooligans is expected to be. (Tough, strong, brutish.) Ask: *How is Hiccup different from this?* (He is small and slight, not strong or intimidating.) *What does Old Wrinkly say about the need for change?* (He suggests that brute force is no longer enough; a future leader will need to be clever and cunning.)
● Can the children suggest which of the boys in Hiccup's group of trainees is more like the typical Hairy Hooligan hero? (Snotlout.)
● Arrange the class into pairs and tell them to fill in photocopiable page 17, comparing Snotlout with Hiccup.
● When they have finished, discuss which qualities Hiccup has that furnish him to be a hero and future leader. (He is clever, uses cunning, has expert knowledge of dragons and Dragonese.)
● Encourage the children to reflect on how Old Wrinkly's words are proved true. They should think about how the adults propose to deal with the Sea Dragon and why a new approach is needed. (Yelling at it or fighting it are futile.) Ask: *What is Hiccup's clever idea?* (He incites the Sea Dragons to fight and kill each other.)

> **Differentiation**
> **For older/more confident learners:** Challenge pairs to discuss how similar or different the Viking idea of a hero is from ours today.
> **For younger/less confident learners:** Let pairs discuss the qualities they think make a hero.

Gobber

> **Objective:** To deduce characters' reasons for behaviour from their actions.
> **What you need:** Copies of *How to Train Your Dragon*, flip chart, individual whiteboards and pens.

What to do

● Tell the children that they are going to focus on the character of Gobber the Belch. Read Chapter 1 at pace. Ask: *What is Gobber's role?* (He is the soldier who trains the boys for their initiation into the tribe.) *What modern-day role does this suggest?* (A sergeant major in charge of army recruits.)
● Brainstorm some words that describe Gobber. (A giant, huge, tough, muscular, loud, scary.) Ask: *How does Gobber speak to the boys?* (He roars at them, insults them, bullies them.)
● Write headings for a three-column table on the flip chart: 'Description', 'Dialogue', 'Action'.
● Arrange the children into small groups and tell them to scan Chapter 1 and find examples about Gobber for each heading. They should note them on their whiteboards. Model examples: 'Description' – *A seven-foot giant with a mad glint in his one working eye*; 'Dialogue' – *SHUDDUP AND GET INTO LINE YOU MISERABLE TADPOLES!*; 'Action' – he spits in the snow.
● When they have finished, invite groups to share their suggestions and write them under the headings on the flip chart. Consider how all three elements build Gobber's character.

> **Differentiation**
> **For older/more confident learners:** Ask the children to expand the table using information from the rest of the novel.
> **For younger/less confident learners:** Invite the children to draw and label a picture of Gobber using information from the table.

Plot, character and setting

Toothless Daydream

> **Objective:** To identify features that writers use to provoke readers' reactions.
> **What you need:** Copies of *How to Train Your Dragon*, flip chart.

What to do
● Tell the children that they are going to focus on the character of Toothless, Hiccup's dragon.
● Arrange the class into small groups. Challenge the groups to think up five descriptive words that could be used about Toothless and write them on their whiteboards. Encourage them to think about his character as well as his appearance. (He is small and scrawny; he is naughty; he is brave, and so on.)
● Bring the class back together and write some of their suggestions on the flip chart. Encourage volunteers from each group to explain why they chose that word, citing evidence from the text to support it. For example: 'Toothless is naughty because he bites Hiccup on the arm', 'Toothless is brave because he flies into the Sea Dragon's nostril'. Record their suggestions and encourage the children to add in further evidence: 'Toothless is naughty because he refuses to catch fish/ provokes Fireworm'.
● Discuss which aspects make Toothless an unlikely hero. Point out that his story is parallel to Hiccup's in that, at first, he is ridiculed for being small, puny and weak but later he redeems himself by showing bravery and selflessness.

> **Differentiation**
> **For older/more confident learners:** Challenge the children to compare and contrast Fireworm with Toothless (refer back to photocopiable page 17).
> **For younger/less confident learners:** Ask the children to divide the statements on the flip chart into two lists: one representing Toothless as an unlikely hero, and the other as a hero.

Useless to Useful

> **Objective:** To identify how different texts are organised.
> **What you need:** Copies of *How to Train Your Dragon*, flip chart, photocopiable page 18, paper.

What to do
● Read at pace the last chapter of the novel. Ask: *What do you feel about the ending? Is it satisfactory? What 'comes right' at the end?* (Toothless is alive and has redeemed himself; Hiccup has proved himself 'useful'.) Ask the children to explain why this is so important for Hiccup. (At the beginning of the story, the other boys dismissed him as 'Hiccup the Useless' and he seemed an unlikely future chief and hero.)
● Discuss what transforms Hiccup from 'Useless' to 'Useful' in the plot, highlighting the sequence of problem and resolution.
● Hand out photocopiable page 18. Ask the children to work in pairs to fill in the boxes, then cut and paste them into the correct order.
● When they have finished, challenge the children to identify which plot elements represent problems and which represent resolutions. Which can be seen as both? (A storm – wakes the Sea Dragons but provides Hiccup with the chance to be a hero; a sneeze – wakes the dragons in the cave, but also saves Hiccup from being swallowed.)

> **Differentiation**
> **For older/more confident learners:** Challenge the children to map the story as a sequence of problems and resolutions.
> **For younger/less confident learners:** Ask the children to think of other significant elements in the plot and add them to the photocopiable sheet.

SECTION
4

The Vikings

● Write down what we learn about Viking life on the island of Berk.

Clothes	Food

Pastimes	Funerals

Religion/Beliefs	Celebrations

Illustration © 2011, Mike Lacey, Beehive Illustration.

The island of Berk

● Complete the page about Berk for a visitors' guide.

A visitors' guide to Berk

Climate and weather
Typical scenery
Local people
Wildlife
Special events
Places to see

Illustration © 2011, Mike Lacey, Beehive Illustration.

Plot, character and setting

Heroes and hooligans

● Compare Hiccup to Snotlout by completing the table below.

	Hiccup	Snotlout
Appearance		
Personality		
Useful skills		
Dragon type		
Best friend		

Plot, character and setting

Useless to Useful

- Explain how each of the following is significant in the plot.
- Cut and paste the boxes in the order they appear in the story.

A feather bomb	A shield
An old joke	A storm
A sneeze	A Roman spear
A Sea Dragon	A test

READ & RESPOND: Activities based on How to Train Your Dragon

Talk about it

Jokes and japes

Objective: To offer reasons and evidence for their views; to respond appropriately to the contributions of others.
What you need: Copies of *How to Train Your Dragon*, flip chart, individual whiteboards and pens.

What to do

● Tell the children that this lesson focuses on humour in the novel. Ask them to suggest what they think makes the novel funny or humorous. Write their suggestions on the flip chart. (Funny events, funny characters, jokes, silly names, comical ideas such as Professor Yobbish's book.)
● Arrange the class into small groups. Assign each group one aspect to research.
● Tell them to scan the novel for examples of their category – so, one group is looking for silly names, another for examples of funny events, and

so on. They should note down their examples on their whiteboards.
● When they have finished, bring the class back together and ask volunteers to provide examples for their category. Write them under the headings on the flip chart.
● Ask the children to nominate the funniest part or aspect of the book, encouraging them to back up their choice with reasons.

Differentiation
For older/more confident learners: Challenge groups to parody the style of humour in their category. For example, they could think of other funny Viking names, or another funny character or event.
For younger/less confident learners: Let groups discuss what they think are the funniest bits of the novel and why.

Dragon profile

Objective: To develop and use specific vocabulary in different contexts.
What you need: Copies of *How to Train Your Dragon*, photocopiable page 22.
Cross-curricular link: Art and design.

What to do

● Discuss which dragon characteristics described in the novel are familiar from other tales/mythology about dragons (they have wings and scales; they breathe fire) and which are invented by the author (they can be trained to hunt fish and deer for their Viking masters; they speak a language called Dragonese).
● Ask the children to cite some of the different species that are described in the novel, from the small, brown dragons that hunt mice to the giant Sea Dragons. Together read the Viking dragon profiles found in Chapters 1 and 2. Ask: *Can you think of other categories for statistics?* (Favourite

foods/diet, likes and dislikes, personality, and so on.) Can they suggest what they would write to describe Toothless under those new headings?
● Arrange the class into small groups and hand out photocopiable page 22. Explain to the children that they are going to invent their own dragon species. They should fill in the profile template and draw and label a sketch of their dragon in the space provided.
● When they have finished, invite volunteers from each group to present the name and key features of their dragon species. Invite the class to vote for the best suggestions.

Differentiation
For older/more confident learners: Ask the children to use the photocopiable sheet to invent another dragon species of their own.
For younger/less confident learners: Invite the children to draw and label a dragon species that they invent or make a model of one.

Talk about it

Bashyball

> **Objective:** To convey detailed information coherently for listeners.
> **What you need:** Copies of *How to Train Your Dragon*, flip chart, individual whiteboards and pens, photocopiable page 23, (optional) images of Aztec/Mayan or other ancient ball sports.
> **Cross-curricular links:** PSHE, history.

What to do
● Ask the children if they can remember the name of the Viking game mentioned in the novel. (Bashyball.) Ask: *What do you imagine this game might be like?* (Hitting or kicking a ball about; fast, rough, dangerous.) Discuss what balls might have been made of long ago (blown up pigs' bladders) and what other equipment might have been used (wooden mallets, leather pads). If possible, show images of early ball games such as Aztec and Mayan Ulama.

● Arrange the children into small groups. Hand out photocopiable page 23 and explain that they are going to describe the game of Bashyball. They will need to describe what kind of ball is used, what other equipment is needed, what the pitch/play area is like, what the rules for scoring are, and so on.
● Allow them time and, when they have finished, invite groups to share their ideas. Write some of the best suggestions on the flip chart.

> **Differentiation**
> **For older/more confident learners:** Challenge groups to plan and present orally a brief match report on a Bashyball game between the Hairy Hooligans and the Meatheads featuring some of the characters from the novel.
> **For younger/less confident learners:** Challenge groups to describe orally the game of Bashyball.

Cliffhangers

> **Objective:** To identify features that writers use to provoke readers' reactions.
> **What you need:** Copies of *How to Train Your Dragon*, flip chart, individual whiteboards and pens.

What to do
● Read aloud the back-cover blurb. Ask: *What are the 'hooks' that make us interested in reading the book?* Suggest that the blurb raises lots of questions (What is the Dragon Initiation Programme? Why does Hiccup have a toothless dragon? What is a Seadragonus Giganticus?) and that it is also written in question form. Point out that we can infer that the hero called Hiccup has to face great challenges and danger, so we wonder if and how he overcomes them.
● Remind the children that cliffhangers are an important feature in adventure stories. They leave questions hanging and so make us want to read on to find out what happens.

● Arrange the class into small groups. Assign each group a few chapters of the novel and tell them to scan through their chapters listing all the page-turners they can find. For example, from the first three chapters they might be: Can the boys catch their dragons and avoid exile? Can they avoid waking the dragons in the cavern? What kind of dragon has Hiccup got in his basket?
● Bring the groups back together and ask for some examples. Discuss how these questions keep us engaged as we read, right to the final cliffhanger – is Toothless really dead?

> **Differentiation**
> **For older/more confident learners:** Challenge groups to plan and present some more questions in the style of the back cover blurb using cliffhangers from the story.
> **For younger/less confident learners:** Let groups discuss what are the most effective cliffhangers in the story and why.

Talk about it

Bully boys

> **Objective:** To empathise with characters and debate moral dilemmas portrayed in texts.
> **What you need:** Copies of *How to Train Your Dragon*, flip chart.
> **Cross-curricular link:** PSHE.

What to do

● Tell the children that they are going to focus on Hiccup's peers, in particular the characters of Snotlout and Dogsbreath. Ask: *In Hiccup's peer group, what sort of characters are Snotlout and Dogsbreath?* (Domineering, bullies.)
● Arrange the children into small groups. Ask them to think of all the ways that Snotlout and Dogsbreath bully Hiccup and Fishlegs and write them down on their whiteboards. (They push them into the snow; they call them insulting names; they threaten them.)
● When they have finished, bring the class back together and discuss the different forms of bullying. Ask: *How do you think Snotlout's bullying makes Hiccup feel?* (Worried, intimidated, inadequate.) *Why does Snotlout think he is superior to Hiccup?* (He is stronger; he is good at Bashyball; his dragon Fireworm is bigger and more successful at hunting than Toothless.)
● Discuss different ways of dealing with bullies. (Ignoring them, facing up to them, telling on them.) Discuss why Hiccup might not be able to go to the adults in his tribe to complain about the bullying. (Because the Hairy Hooligans admire brute force, physical strength, and so on.)
● Do the children think that Hiccup gets the better of the bullies in the end, and if so how? (He wins their respect because he saves the tribe.)

> **Differentiation**
> **For older/more confident learners:** Let groups discuss how and why the dynamics of Hiccup's peer group change over the course of the story.
> **For younger/less confident learners:** Let groups discuss the problem of bullying and what the best ways of dealing with it are.

Dragon motivation

> **Objective:** To interrogate texts to deepen and clarify understanding and response.
> **What you need:** Copies of *How to Train Your Dragon*, flip chart, photocopiable page 24.
> **Cross-curricular link:** PSHE.

What to do

● Tell the children that in this lesson they are going to explore how Hiccup manages to train Toothless against all the odds.
● Challenge them to list all the methods of training that Hiccup tries with Toothless that fail. (Bribery, yelling, revenge, greed, and so on.) Write their suggestions on the flip chart.
● Discuss how Hiccup slowly builds Toothless' loyalty so that, in the end, Toothless goes against dragon nature and performs a selfless act to rescue Hiccup. (He talks to him in Dragonese; looks after him; feeds him lobsters; doesn't shout at him; tells him jokes; lets him sleep in his bed and so on.) Write their suggestions on the flip chart.
● Hand out photocopiable page 24 and tell the children to work in pairs to complete the sections.
● Bring the class back together and discuss why they think Hiccup's training works when yelling doesn't.

> **Differentiation**
> **For older/more confident learners:** Let the children discuss what they would include in a definitive list for 'dragon motivation' given Hiccup's results.
> **For younger/less confident learners:** Let children discuss the qualities that Hiccup brings to training Toothless (patience, care, commitment, thought).

Talk about it

SECTION
5

Dragon profile

- Complete the profile for your own new species of dragon.

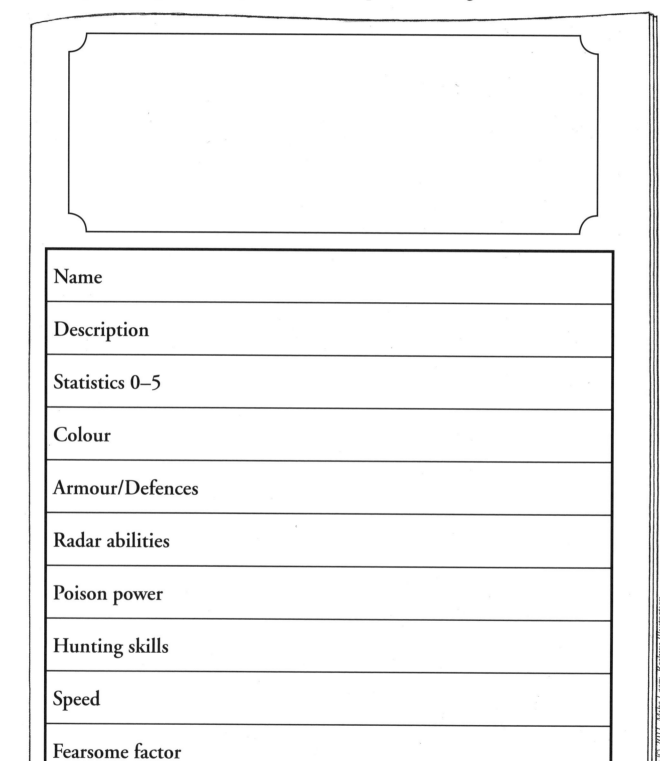

Name	
Description	
Statistics 0–5	
Colour	
Armour/Defences	
Radar abilities	
Poison power	
Hunting skills	
Speed	
Fearsome factor	

Illustration © 2011, Mike Lacey, Beehive Illustration.

SCHOLASTIC
www.scholastic.co.uk

READ & RESPOND: Activities based on How to Train Your Dragon

Bashyball

● What do you imagine the game of Bashyball would be like? Describe it below.

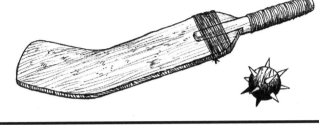

Describe the ball and any other kit or equipment needed.
Describe the pitch or play area.
Team/players
Explain how the game is played.
What are the rules for scoring or winning?

Talk about it

SECTION
5

Dragon motivation

● Explain the results of these training methods on Toothless and rate how effective they are.

Method	Result	0–5 rating
Fear		
Greed		
Vanity		
Revenge		
Jokes		

● Write down three ways that Hiccup builds Toothless' loyalty.

1 _____

_____

2 _____

_____

3 _____

_____

READ & RESPOND: Activities based on How to Train Your Dragon

Get writing

Songs and riddles

Objective: To show imagination through language used to create emphasis, humour, atmosphere or suspense.
What you need: Copies of *How to Train Your Dragon*, examples of 'What am I?' riddles, flip chart, whiteboards and pens.

What to do

● Read aloud the Sea Dragon's supper song in Hiccup's epilogue. Ask: *Who is singing? Which clues tell you this identity? Why is this a fitting/poetic ending?* (The fiery breath, name of Death.)
● Discuss the riddle form of the Sea Dragon's song. Write some 'What am I?' riddles on the flip chart for the children to answer. For example:
   ● Food feeds me. Water kills me. What am I? (Fire.)
   ● I have a face but no head. I have three hands but no feet. What am I? (A clock.)

● Explain that the Vikings often used riddles or kennings to describe things. Kennings are descriptive compound words, such as 'spear trees' for warriors and 'whale road' for the ocean.
● In pairs, the children should brainstorm some words and kennings describing the features of a character from the book. For Toothless, perhaps: 'one-tooth', 'mischievous', 'plucky'. They can try combining words to form kennings: 'one-tooth torpedo', 'lobster muncher'. They should go on to write a riddle using the supper song as a model.
● Bring the class back together and ask pairs to present their kennings and riddles, challenging the class to identify the characters described.

Differentiation
For older/more confident learners: Pairs can write more kennings or riddle songs for other characters.
For younger/less confident learners: Model a riddle song for one of the characters to get them started.

The name game

Objective: To show imagination through language used to create emphasis, humour, atmosphere or suspense.
What you need: Copies of *How to Train Your Dragon*, flip chart, individual whiteboards and pens.

What to do

● Tell the children that they are going to focus on the funny names in the novel and try to think up some funny names of their own. Begin by writing headings for name categories on the flip chart: 'Dragons', 'Dragon species', 'Tribes', 'Characters'. Then ask the children to recall some names from the novel for each category. Write them under their headings.
● Discuss what makes the names funny and effective: techniques (alliteration), rude or funny words (belch), parodying Viking name forms with epithets (Gobber the Belch).
● Arrange the children into pairs and challenge

them to think of some more names to go in each category. They should start by brainstorming descriptive words. For example, for the character names they might write 'fearless', 'massive', 'mouthy', 'grotesque'. They should also use alliteration where possible. For example, a character might be called 'Malcolm the Mouthy', or 'George the Gross'; a tribe might be the 'Gormless Geeks'.
● When they have written some ideas for each category on their whiteboards, bring the class back together and encourage pairs to share their ideas.

Differentiation
For older/more confident learners: Challenge the children to work independently to think up some more names in each category.
For younger/less confident learners: Provide lists of descriptive words as a resource to help the children invent names.

Get writing

Viking pals' page

Objective: To show imagination through language used to create emphasis, humour, atmosphere or suspense.
What you need: Copies of *How to Train Your Dragon*, photocopiable page 28, flip chart.
Cross-curricular link: PSHE.

What to do
● Tell the children that in this lesson they are going to focus on the character of Gobber the Belch, and plan his profile for a social networking page. Ask the children to summarise their impressions of Gobber. (Huge, physically powerful, tough, a sergeant major type, a bit of a bully, and so on.)
● Challenge the children to recall any details about Gobber that help to reveal his character.

(The clothes he wears; the language he typically uses; the fact that he stole the library book, and so on.) Write their suggestions on the flip chart.
● Arrange the children in pairs and hand out photocopiable page 28. Tell them to imagine they are Gobber preparing his profile for a Viking social networking site. They should fill in the sheet to reflect his personality.

Differentiation
For older/more confident learners: Challenge the children to compile a profile for another character from the novel using the photocopiable sheet.
For younger/less confident learners: Discuss Gobber's character in more detail and note key points on the flip chart before the children attempt the photocopiable sheet.

The Berk Herald

Objective: To write non-narrative text types using structures of different text types.
What you need: Copies of *How to Train Your Dragon*, individual whiteboards and pens, photocopiable page 29.
Cross-curricular links: Citizenship, ICT.

What to do
● Ask the children to close their eyes and visualise the scene as you read aloud the passage in Chapter 13 from *The trail up to the Highest Point* to *Two not enough for you?* Challenge them to recall some of the details (the dolphins' bones, scallop shells, shipwreck, violet plumes of smoke).
● Explain that they are going to imagine that they are a journalist working for the local Viking newspaper, *The Berk Herald*. They are going to write a report about the discovery of the Purple Death Sea Dragon, and report on events so far.

● Arrange the children in pairs. Tell them to scan Chapters 11 and 12, noting down the main events on their whiteboards. (Two huge dragons land on The Long Beach after a bad storm; one eats the other; the Council of War meets, and so on.)
● Hand out photocopiable page 29 and ask pairs to complete the sheet as a news report. They should headline the discovery of the Purple Death and report the main events that have happened since the Sea Dragons first arrived on The Long Beach.

Differentiation
For older/more confident learners: Children could develop their news reports using ICT skills.
For younger/less confident learners: Give support by highlighting the main events in Chapters 11 and 12 for the children to include in their reports.

Get writing

Thor'sday Thursday

> **Objective:** To write non-narrative text types using structures of different text types.
> **What you need:** Copies of *How to Train Your Dragon*, individual whiteboards and pens.

What to do

● Read the first part of Chapter 10 as far as *his traditional appearance at the Thor'sday Thursday celebrations*. Ask: *Who is Thor?* (The Viking god of thunder.) Elicit that our word 'Thursday' is named after Thor, who was believed to create thunder with a giant hammer.

● Focus on the programme of events, asking volunteers to read out each activity. Highlight the humour in the gross and comical ideas and ironic language, such as *the delicate art of fighting with axes*. Invite suggestions for prizes in the raffle, and what they imagine the closing ceremony might be like.

● Arrange the class into small groups. Tell the children that they are going to invent another activity that might feature on the programme and write a listing for it following the style in the novel. Encourage them to brainstorm ideas first, using their knowledge of what the Viking tribes in the novel admire (rough or violent sports, bloodthirsty contests).

● Allow them time to plan and draft their idea, then invite volunteers from each group to read them aloud. Encourage feedback and take a class vote on the best and most convincing event/activity.

> **Differentiation**
> **For older/more confident learners:** Challenge the children to write some more activities or ideas for stalls independently and write programme listings for them.
> **For younger/less confident learners:** Let the children use ideas from the novel (juggling, fortune-telling) and write programme listings for them.

True reviews

> **Objective:** To write non-narrative texts using structures of different text types.
> **What you need:** Copies of *How to Train Your Dragon* and photocopiable page 30.

What to do

● Tell the children that they are going to focus on the book within a book, Professor Yobbish's '*How to Train Your Dragon*'. Look together at the book content, interrogating the text and highlighting the jokes contained in it: the award, publishers, price, and so on.

● Focus on the book reviews. Highlight the sources: newspapers, magazines, a well-known commentator. Discuss the anomaly between their enthusiastic praise – *sensitive and well-researched* – and the reality of the book's content. Discuss some of the key charges against it. (It only contains one rule; *Yell at it* is a simplistic rule that doesn't always work; there is no research or evidence cited, and so on.)

● Tell the children that they are going to write some more reviews which give a truthful appraisal of the book. Hand out photocopiable page 30 and allow time for completion.

> **Differentiation**
> **For older/more confident learners:** Challenge the children to suggest some more titles that Big Axe Books might publish.
> **For younger/less confident learners:** Children can work in pairs to complete the photocopiable sheet.

Get writing

SECTION
6

Viking pals' page

● Plan Gobber's profile for a Viking social networking site.

Hello, my name is

_____

Where I live

_____

My occupation

_____

The best word to
describe me is

Typical words or phrases I use

_____

My super power

_____

My guilty pleasure

_____

Three things I plan to do before I die:

1 _____

_____

2 _____

_____

3 _____

_____

Get writing

SECTION
6

The Berk Herald

● Write a headline about the discovery of the Purple Death and then report key events that have happened since the Sea Dragons first appeared.

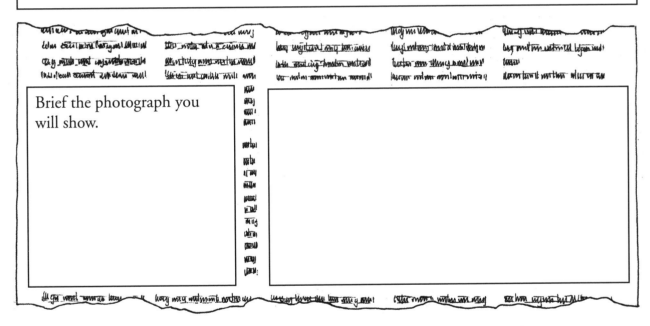

Brief the photograph you will show.

● Write some quotes by local people about the events described.

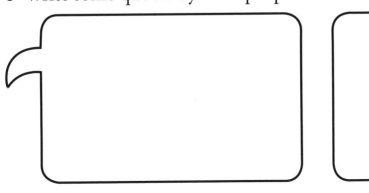

Illustrations © 2011, Mike Lacey, Beehive Illustration.

Get writing

SECTION

6

True reviews

- Write some truthful reviews for Professor Yobbish's book.

Reviewer	Comment

- Comment on these claims.

Claim	Comment
'Hugely entertaining and informative'	
'Sensitive and well-researched'	
'The culmination of his research'	
'The definitive textbook on the subject'	
'Look inside for ALL the answers'	

PHOTOCOPIABLE

READ & RESPOND: Activities based on *How to Train Your Dragon*

Assessment

Assessment advice

Over the course of these lessons, children carry out a range of activities to exercise their speaking, listening, reading and writing skills. Assessment should be an ongoing process, regularly recording progress and highlighting areas that need improvement. It should be based on contributions in shared class work as well as on written individual, paired or group work.

Begin each lesson by explaining the learning objective and, where possible, relate it to other literacy and cross-curricular work. At the end of the lesson, encourage the children to assess their own work against the objectives set, and to decide which areas need further practice. They should also be encouraged to provide constructive feedback for writing partners and groups.

The children can create their own assessment activities – for example, working in groups to devise multiple-choice or true or false quizzes about the novel. They could compile spelling tests based on themes or topics (dragons, the island of Berk) or parts of speech (verbs, nouns, adjectives). Photocopiable page 32 invites children to reflect on story genre and key themes and can be used as an assessment activity.

What's the story?

> **Objective:** To interrogate texts to deepen and clarify understanding and response.
> **What you need:** Flip chart, photocopiable page 32.

What to do

● Encourage the children to say whether they enjoyed *How to Train Your Dragon* and, if so, why. Discuss their favourite aspects of the story. Ask: *Which bits were most memorable? Why? What made you want to read on?*

● Have any of them read any other novels in the Hiccup series and, if so, which do they like best and why? Have any of them seen the film animation of the novel and, if so, do they think it was a good adaptation? Can they recall what was similar/different (plot line, characters) in the book and film versions? Ask the children to suggest why film-makers might have been keen to adapt the novel. (A fast-moving, exciting plot; a sympathetic hero; the visual potential of the fantasy element with the dragons/dragon fights; the humour of the story.)

● Discuss together the genre of the novel. Do the children think it is primarily an adventure story, a humorous story or a fantasy? Ask them to identify different elements of each within the novel and write their suggestions under headings for each genre on the flip chart.

● Encourage the children to reflect on special text features within the novel, such as the use of a different font for Dragonese; different text types such as dragon species definitions, a programme of events, a letter, a library book, and so on. What do the children think these contribute and which genre do they fit best in? Focus on the illustrations and, again, encourage the children to think what they contribute. Does the doodle/scribble style suit the novel and if so why?

● Let the children work on their own to complete photocopiable page 32, using their knowledge of *How to Train Your Dragon*.

What's the story?

● Explain three ways that *How to Train Your Dragon* fits into the adventure genre.

1. _____

2. _____

3. _____

● Which other genres could it also belong to?

Genre	Yes/No	Evidence
Memoir/ Autobiography		
Historical novel		
Humorous novel		
Fantasy novel		
Realistic novel		

● Choose three key themes and say how they feature in the novel.

Friendship   Bullying   Growing up   Leadership Facing fears   Viking values   Heroism

1. _____

2. _____

3. _____